# FORZA

# HORIZON

# 6

# GAME

# GUIDE

# Table of Contents

# CHAPTER 1: INTRODUCTION TO FORZA HORIZON 6

## 1.1 Overview of the Game World & Theme

Welcome to Forza Horizon 6, the next evolution of the open-world racing franchise known for its stunning visuals, seamless multiplayer, and deep car culture. In FH6, players are thrown into an exhilarating, ever-changing festival of speed set in the most immersive map the series has ever seen.

A New Location, A New Horizon

This time around, the Horizon Festival takes us to Japan — a fan-favorite destination that offers a rich blend of tradition and technology. From neon-lit cityscapes of Tokyo-inspired regions to tranquil mountain passes and countryside villages, the game world is as diverse as it is massive.

Expect:

- Winding touge roads for drift battles.
- Bustling urban centers with tight streets perfect for street racing.
- Serene rural areas where cherry blossoms and rice paddies set the stage for scenic cruises.
- Mountain terrain and coastal highways for high-speed challenges.

Theme: Culture Meets Competition

Forza Horizon 6 embraces the theme of "Culture Meets Competition." The game doesn't just throw you into races—it immerses you in the automotive lifestyle of Japan:

- Car meets in parking garages.
- Street art and customization hubs.
- Authentic local music and ambient soundscapes.

You'll see influences from real-world car culture movements like JDM (Japanese Domestic Market) tuning, drift scenes, and even Bosozoku-style customization.

Evolving World, Live Festival

The world of FH6 is alive and always changing:

- A seasonal system returns, but with more localized weather effects (foggy mountains, typhoons, snowfall).
- Live in-game events like street meets and illegal night races pop up on your map.
- AI and multiplayer events blend together, creating a near-seamless online/offline world.

Freedom at Your Pace

As always, you decide how to play. Whether you're:

- Grinding leaderboards,
- Building the ultimate drift machine,
- Tuning a retro ride,
- Or just exploring and photographing landscapes…

## 1.2 Key New Features in FH6

Forza Horizon 6 takes everything fans loved about its predecessors and builds on it with bold innovations, deeper customization, and more immersive gameplay mechanics. Whether you're a competitive racer or a casual cruiser, FH6 introduces fresh systems and enhancements that redefine the open-world racing experience.

1. Revamped Physics & Handling Engine

- The driving model has been significantly refined, providing more realistic tire grip, suspension movement, and road feel.
- Different surfaces like gravel, wet pavement, and snow react more naturally.
- Car weight, aerodynamics, and drivetrain have a bigger impact on how each vehicle handles—greatly improving the depth of simulation.

2. Hyper-Detailed World with Procedural Weather

- FH6 introduces dynamic microclimates. You can start a race under the sun and finish in a rainstorm, or find fog rolling in over a mountain pass.
- Each biome (urban, forest, mountain, coastal) has unique weather systems and environmental hazards (like flooding, falling leaves, or icy roads).
- Enhanced day-night lighting and ray-traced reflections make every moment photo-worthy.

3. Immersive Storylines & Character Interaction

- Horizon Stories are now branching narratives with dialogue choices, voice-acted characters, and reputations.
- You'll partner with in-game characters to unlock exclusive missions, like drifting school with a local legend or off-road expeditions with influencers.
- Character creation has been expanded, with more customization and emotive cutscenes.

4. Next-Gen Customization Systems

- Garage 2.0 brings deeper tuning options and full visual overhaul capabilities:
    - Custom engine swaps, drivetrain conversions, active aero tuning.
    - New vinyl layering tools and paint effects like metallic flake, matte blends, and reactive neon underglow.
- Blueprint 2.0 lets players build multi-stage events with unique rulesets, custom weather, and scripted AI behavior.

5. Integrated Multiplayer Evolution

- "Horizon Live" mode allows for drop-in multiplayer without loading screens or menus.
- PvP and Co-op are seamlessly integrated into the game world—races, challenges, and car meets can happen organically while free-roaming.
- A new social reputation system rewards clean racing, creativity in designs, and community interaction.

## 1.3 Game Modes: Solo, Co-Op, Multiplayer

Forza Horizon 6 continues the series' legacy of offering a dynamic and flexible gameplay structure that caters to all types of racers—whether you're a solo explorer, a co-op challenger, or a PvP adrenaline junkie. This chapter breaks down the core game modes and how they tie into the seamless open-world experience.

Solo Mode: Your Horizon, Your Pace

Perfect for players who prefer a laid-back, personal experience.

- Story Campaigns & Horizon Adventures
  Progress through multiple narrative arcs, each themed around a part of Japanese car culture: drifting, off-roading, street racing, etc.
  Choices made during missions can unlock special events, characters, or exclusive cars.
- Map Exploration & World Activities
  Discover hidden roads, scenic views, and collectibles like bonus boards or Barn Finds at your own pace.
- Time Trials & Custom Events
  Set personal records on Drift Zones, Speed Traps, Danger Signs, and more. Try user-created races via the Blueprint system.

Co-Op Mode: Drive Together, Win Together

Team up with friends or other players to complete events and challenges.

- Horizon Stories in Co-Op
  Tackle story missions as a squad. Dialogue and cutscenes adapt based on group participation.
- Shared World Exploration
  Cruise, drift, or complete objectives together without needing to enter lobbies.
- Co-Op Racing Events
  Join as a convoy and race against AI teams. Wins are collective—perfect for casual group play or friend groups of mixed skill levels.

Multiplayer (PvP): The Competitive Side of Horizon

For those who want to test their skills against real players.

- Horizon Open
  Drop into live PvP events including circuit races, sprints, drift contests, and even demolition derbies. Skill-based matchmaking keeps things fair.
- The Eliminator: Battle Royale Returns
  A fan-favorite mode where 70+ players compete in an ever-closing map. Eliminate opponents in head-to-head sprints, upgrade your car, and survive to win.
- Horizon Cup: Ranked Racing
  A new structured PvP mode with weekly tournaments, seasonal leaderboards, and rewards like exclusive liveries and cars.
- Community Events & Live Challenges
  Flash mobs of races and stunts that pop up in-world and encourage spontaneous competition with nearby players.

Cross-Mode Progression

- Everything you do—whether solo, co-op, or multiplayer—contributes to your overall Festival progress, XP, and rewards.
- FH6 supports crossplay across Xbox, PC, and cloud platforms, ensuring you can join your friends no matter where they're racing from.

## 1.4 Tips for Beginners: What to Know Before You Start

Just fired up *Forza Horizon 6* for the first time? You're in for a thrill — but don't worry, we've got your back. Whether you're new to the series or just need a refresher, this chapter walks you through key starter tips that will help you hit the ground drifting.

1. Learn the Ropes with Assists On

- Forza Horizon 6 gives you full control over driving assists — traction control, stability, braking, steering, etc.
- Don't feel bad about using them at first. Turn on automatic braking and steering assist if you're brand new.
- As you improve, slowly turn off assists to get better rewards and experience the full potential of your car.

2. Don't Rush to Buy Cars

- You'll earn a ton of cars naturally through events, wheelspins, and seasonal rewards.
- Stick with a few starter cars and focus on upgrading them instead of buying new ones early on.

- Try different car types (off-road, JDM, hypercars) through loaner cars in early events — this helps you find what suits your style.

## 3. Explore Early and Often

- The map is packed with things to discover: Barn Finds, XP boards, hidden roads, photo spots.
- Drive off the main roads — there's no penalty for going off-track. Sometimes, the best rewards are hidden in forests or behind buildings.
- Unlock Fast Travel points by smashing billboards and visiting key locations — it'll save you hours later.

## 4. Use the Rewind Feature (It's Not Cheating!)

- Messed up a turn? Flew off a cliff mid-drift? Rewind lets you undo mistakes without restarting the whole race.
- Tap the rewind button (usually ←◻ or 'R' on keyboard) to go back a few seconds and try again.
- It's a great learning tool — use it to experiment with braking zones or new techniques.

## Bonus Beginner Tips:

- Check the Festival Playlist weekly for easy rewards like rare cars and cash.
- Try everything once — showcase events, stories, stunts, even photo challenges. They help you level up and learn mechanics.
- Don't forget to claim your daily/weekly Wheelspins — they're free and often give you cars, credits, or emotes.

# CHAPTER 2: GETTING STARTED

## 2.1 Choosing Your First Car

Your first car in *Forza Horizon 6* sets the tone for how you'll experience the early game. While you'll unlock more vehicles quickly, your initial pick should reflect your driving style and comfort level.

Starter Car Options

FH6 offers a selection of starter cars across multiple categories—typically a balanced street racer, an agile hatchback, and a rugged off-roader. Each has pros and cons:

- Street Racer (e.g., Nissan 350Z)
  Great for speed, drifting, and early race events. Low ground clearance makes it weaker off-road.
- Hatchback (e.g., VW Golf GTI)
  Beginner-friendly, nimble handling. Excels in city events and tight circuits.
- Off-Roader (e.g., Ford Bronco or Toyota Land Cruiser)
  Handles dirt roads, hills, and exploration like a champ. Slower on asphalt but perfect for discovery.

What to Consider

- Handling vs. Speed – Beginners often benefit from a stable, well-handling car rather than a fast but slippery one.

- Terrain Versatility – Consider what kind of events you'll do first. FH6's diverse landscape makes all-terrain capability handy.
- Upgrade Potential – Some starter cars have better upgrade trees and tuning potential than others.

Pro Tip: Don't stress too hard — you'll earn enough credits (CR) and Wheelspins to fill your garage quickly.

## 2.2 Understanding Car Classes and Performance Stats

Each car in *Forza Horizon 6* is categorized by class and rated by a Performance Index (PI). These indicators help you quickly compare cars and pick the right one for the event ahead.

Car Classes Explained

Classes range from the slowest to the most elite performers:

- D-Class (PI 100–499): Older or basic cars — good for novelty races or fun builds.
- C-Class (PI 500–599): Slow but stable—great for early-game or tuning practice.
- B-Class (PI 600–699): Solid all-rounders—ideal for most general races.
- A-Class (PI 700–799): Where things start getting fast—balanced and fun.
- S1-Class (PI 800–899): High-performance—good for serious racing and PvP.
- S2-Class (PI 900–998): Hypercars and exotic monsters.
- X-Class (PI 999): Maxed-out machines—usually post-upgrade or Blueprint-only.

Key Stats to Watch

Each car has base stats you'll see on the selection screen:

- Speed – Straight-line max velocity.
- Acceleration – How fast it hits high speed.
- Handling – Cornering ability and responsiveness.
- Braking – How quickly it slows down.
- Off-Road – Important for dirt, snow, or trail events.

Pro Tip: Don't just look at the PI — the type of event matters more. A C-Class off-roader will beat an S1 hypercar in a mountain trail event.

## 2.3 UI and HUD Navigation

*Forza Horizon 6*'s user interface is clean but packed with features. Understanding the layout will help you access everything from races to custom liveries without frustration.

Main Menu Overview

- Map – Your go-to for setting routes, finding races, locating Barn Finds, and discovering hidden roads.
- Cars – Access your garage, car mastery, upgrades, and customization.
- Festival Playlist – Seasonal objectives, challenges, and limited-time rewards.
- Horizon Adventure – Campaign missions and story paths.
- Online – Multiplayer races, The Eliminator, Horizon Tour, and car meets.
- Settings – Control mapping, assists, graphics, and more.

In-Race HUD (Heads-Up Display)

- Speedometer & Tachometer – Bottom right. Shows your speed, gear, and RPM.
- Mini-Map – Bottom left. Displays your route, nearby players, and objectives.
- Race Info – Top middle. Shows position, laps, checkpoints, and time.
- Telemetry (Optional) – For advanced tuning, real-time feedback on suspension, tire grip, and forces.

Notification System

- Top left alerts: New challenges, Wheelspins, accolades, or unlocked events.
- Quick tips: Pop up contextually to teach new mechanics or shortcuts.

Navigation Pro Tips

- Use the filter system on the map to declutter and find what you need (races only, collectibles, story missions, etc.).
- Press and hold the right stick (RS) on controllers to reset your camera or re-center the map quickly.

## 2.4 Setting Up Driving Assists and Controls

Your control setup can completely change how enjoyable FH6 feels — especially when you're just getting started or experimenting with competitive modes.

Driving Assists Menu

From the "Settings" menu, go to Difficulty & Assists to adjust:

- Steering –
    - *Auto*: Handles steering for you.
    - *Normal*: Recommended for beginners.
    - *Simulation*: For purists—harder to control but realistic.
- Braking –
    - *Auto Braking*: Good for learning corners.
    - *ABS On*: Prevents wheels from locking during hard braking.
- Traction & Stability Control – Helps prevent skidding or spinning out.
- Driving Line –
    - *Full*: Great learning tool, shows optimal path and braking zones.
    - *Braking Only*: Less intrusive if you already know track layouts.

Recommendation for Beginners:
Start with Normal Steering, ABS On, and Traction Control On.
Gradually reduce assists as you gain confidence.

Controller & Keyboard Mapping

- Supports full controller remapping (Xbox, PS via streaming, etc.).
- Includes presets for wheel setups (Logitech, Thrustmaster, Fanatec).
- On keyboard, consider using manual shifting keys if you're using clutch setups.

Sensitivity & Dead Zones

- Adjust steering sensitivity if your turns feel too twitchy or sluggish.
- Modify dead zones to tune how much stick movement registers input — especially important for fine-tuning analog triggers or wheels.

Custom Presets

- You can save multiple control setups — perfect if you switch between racing styles (e.g., drifting vs. off-road rally).

# CHAPTER 3: EXPLORING THE MAP

## 3.1 Region Breakdown: Biomes & Cities

*Forza Horizon 6* takes place in a richly detailed open world inspired by Japan — blending real-world geography with fantasy-level driving experiences. Understanding the landscape is crucial for choosing the right cars, navigating efficiently, and completing challenges.

Mountain Region – Mt. Akuma Pass

- Twisty mountain roads perfect for drifting, touge racing, and scenic views.
- Weather often includes fog and snow, adding challenge to higher elevations.
- Home to hillclimb events, drift zones, and hidden collectibles in tunnels and shrines.

City Region – Shirokawa & Higashi Port

- Shirokawa is a modern metropolis, filled with skyscrapers, neon-lit roads, and tight alleyways.
- Higashi Port features industrial zones, shipping containers, and complex overpasses.
- Great for street racing, night events, and capturing photo challenges with city lights.

Coastal Region – Sakura Shores

- Wide, curving roads alongside ocean cliffs.

- Mixed-terrain driving: asphalt highways meet sandy beaches and boardwalks.
- Ideal for speed zones, danger signs, and casual cruising.

Countryside – Rice Fields & Shrines

- Lush rural areas filled with rice terraces, bamboo forests, and historic temples.
- Includes gravel paths and muddy roads — perfect for off-road racing and exploration.
- Features plenty of Barn Finds, including classic JDM cars.

Volcanic Zone – Blackstone Ridge

- A more extreme, rugged terrain with lava rock roads, canyons, and geysers.
- Home to high-stakes events like The Gauntlet and Eliminator arenas.
- Visually stunning but dangerous—bring an AWD beast.

## 3.2 Fast Travel, Garage Locations & Outposts

Efficient movement and resource access are key to making the most of your time in FH6. This section outlines how to move faster, switch cars, and manage your builds without wasting time.

Fast Travel System

- Initially limited—you can only fast travel to Festival Sites, Outposts, and Homes.
- Fast Travel Boards (smashable signs) scattered across the map reduce cost per jump.
    - Smash all 50 to unlock free fast travel anywhere.

- Upgrade your fast travel perks via the Car Mastery tree or Player Perks.

## Garage Locations

- Garages allow you to access your full car collection, upgrade parts, and tune builds.
- You can store cars at:
    - Festival HQs (main campaign locations).
    - Player Homes (purchasable with in-game CR).
    - Outposts unlocked across biomes.
- Each garage can also house a Quick Upgrade bay and Blueprint creation terminal.

## Outposts (Horizon Satellites)

- Mini-hubs located in remote or biome-specific regions.
- Offer access to basic services: car switching, repairs, fast travel, and local events.
- Often serve as starting points for cross-country races or story arcs tied to their location (e.g., a drifting dojo in the mountains).

## Using Homes for Strategy

- Buying homes isn't just cosmetic—they come with perks like:
    - Extra Wheelspins
    - Fast travel bonuses
    - Daily reward boosts
    - Custom spawn points — super helpful for race farming or challenge grinding

## 3.3 Dynamic Weather & Time-of-Day Effects

One of the biggest immersive strengths of *Forza Horizon 6* is its living world, where weather and time aren't just visual — they directly affect gameplay, strategy, and the overall experience.

Dynamic Time-of-Day

- Time passes naturally, creating sunrises, high noon, sunsets, and deep night cycles.
- Certain races or collectibles may only appear during specific times (e.g., night-only street events).
- Use Photo Mode to pause time and capture scenic shots — golden hour in FH6 is stunning.

Pro Tip: Time cycles reset with some online events. Plan exploration during daylight for easier navigation.

Seasonal Weather System

- FH6 continues the weekly rotating season system (Spring, Summer, Autumn, Winter), each lasting ~7 days in real-world time.
- Each season changes:
  - Weather conditions
  - Water levels and terrain grip
  - Event types and rewards

| Season | Features |
|--------|----------|
| Spring | Rain showers, blooming cherry trees, slippery asphalt |
| Summer | Hot, dry roads with high visibility and top speeds |

| Autumn | Wet roads, falling leaves, strong winds in coastal zones |
| Winter | Snow in the mountains, frozen lakes, icy off-road routes |

Weather Effects on Gameplay

- Rain & wet conditions reduce grip — even on supercars.
- Snow or mud changes tire effectiveness. Equip off-road tires or AWD in advance.
- Fog affects visibility during high-speed runs — especially at dawn in mountain regions.

Tuning for the Weather

- Always check the Festival Playlist or Season Preview before customizing your build.
- Install rain tires, switch to snow-ready AWD setups, or tune your aerodynamics to handle windy drift zones.

## 3.4 Finding Hidden Roads and Landmarks

FH6's map is packed with secrets, from scenic shrines to underground passages — and you're rewarded for finding them.

Hidden Roads & Bonus Routes

- Roads that don't appear on the map until driven are counted toward Road Discovery Progress.
- Includes:
  - Back alleys in Shirokawa
  - Jungle trails in the countryside

   o Rooftop shortcuts in the port city

## Barn Finds

- Classic JDM and concept cars are hidden in remote barns — unlocked after hearing rumors through exploration or story missions.
- Once discovered, the barn is marked and the car is restored over time.
- You can accelerate restoration using credits.

Some Barn Finds are season-locked — meaning you can only get them during specific weather cycles.

## Landmarks to Watch For

- Scattered around the map are:
  - Temples – Often tied to photo challenges or story events.
  - Lighthouses & Pagodas – Fast travel spots or Barn Find clues.
  - Abandoned rail lines, tunnels, shrines – Often hiding bonus boards or alternate race starts.

## Collectibles

- XP Boards – Smash to earn experience.
- Fast Travel Boards – Reduce fast travel costs (50 total).
- Treasure Hunts – Solve riddles to earn rare cars and large credit payouts.
- Photo Challenges – Take specific pictures at locations or with themed vehicles.

# CHAPTER 4: THE CARS OF FH6

## 4.1 Categories: Off-Road, Hypercars, Classics & More

*Forza Horizon 6* features hundreds of cars across different categories, each suited for specific terrains and race types. Knowing the categories will help players build balanced collections and compete effectively.

Main Car Categories

- Off-Road / Rally
    - High ground clearance, AWD, built for dirt, gravel, and snow.
    - Great for Trail Blazers, Cross Country, and seasonal challenges.
- Hypercars / Supercars
    - Extremely high speed, acceleration, and handling.
    - Ideal for road races, speed traps, and speed zones on highways.
- Classics / Retro
    - Iconic vehicles from the '60s to '90s, including JDM legends and muscle cars.
    - Often needed for specialty events or seasonal challenges.
- Muscle / Drag
    - Raw power, especially in straight lines.
    - Dominant in 1/4-mile races and showdowns.
- Street / Hatchbacks
    - Agile and quick, perfect for urban circuits and tight tracks.
    - Excellent for new players and city-based events.

Specialty Classes

- Drift Cars – Tuned for oversteer and style-based events.
- Buggies & Trophy Trucks – Great for sand dunes and jumps.
- EVs (Electric Vehicles) – Instant torque and quiet, futuristic performance.

## 4.2 How to Unlock and Purchase Cars

FH6 offers many ways to expand your garage — from buying to winning, and even discovering.

Ways to Get Cars

- Autoshow – The in-game dealership. Buy any non-exclusive car with CR (Credits).
- Wheelspins / Super Wheelspins – Win random vehicles, credits, or cosmetics.
- Festival Playlist – Weekly challenges offer exclusive and seasonal cars.
- Barn Finds – Hidden classics that are restored over time.
- Auction House – Player-to-player marketplace for rare or tuned cars.
- Car Pass & DLC – Paid content adds new cars weekly or via bundles.

Currency & Rarity

- CR (Credits) – Main in-game currency, earned from races, challenges, and sales.
- Exclusive Cars – Only available via events, milestones, or limited-time drops.

- Legendary / Rare Tags – Color-coded in the garage to show scarcity.

## 4.3 Car Masteries & Custom Perks

Each car comes with a Mastery Tree, letting you spend Skill Points earned from stunts, races, and combos.

How Car Masteries Work

- Earn Skill Points through driving feats (drifts, jumps, near-misses, etc.).
- Spend them on perks tied to each specific car — these vary widely.

Common Mastery Perks

- Skill Boosts – Increases combo duration or multiplier.
- XP or CR Bonuses – One-time or permanent increases.
- Wheelspins – Often found deep in the tree, great for building wealth.
- Fast Travel Discounts – Reduce travel costs with certain vehicles.

Tuning Your Mastery Strategy

- Prioritize cars with Wheelspin perks for maximum value.
- Build stunt-focused cars with extended skill chains for easier mastery farming.
- Some cars have unique perks, like unlocking hidden vehicles or cosmetics.

## 4.4 Performance Upgrades vs. Aesthetic Mods

Customization is at the heart of FH6. You can tweak how your car looks, handles, and performs with separate upgrade paths.

Performance Upgrades

Accessed via the Upgrades & Tuning menu, these affect your car's stats and PI class:

- Engine Swaps – Drastically boost power; can change the car's class.
- Drivetrain Conversions – Switch FWD ↔ AWD for better handling or traction.
- Tires & Suspension – Crucial for terrain-specific builds (e.g., rally vs. drag).
- Weight Reduction – Improves acceleration and handling.
- Turbo/Superchargers – Big boost in speed; may require tune balancing.

Aesthetic Mods

- Visual Upgrades – Body kits, wings, bumpers, and hoods.
- Paint & Vinyl Editor – Fully custom liveries or download community-made ones.
- Rims & Tires – Change size and style without affecting performance.
- Window Tint, Engine Bay, Lights – Just for show, but add style points.

Blueprint Tuning

Advanced players can use the tuning section to adjust:

- Gear ratios
- Tire pressure
- Aero balance
- Differential behavior

# CHAPTER 5: RACING AND EVENTS

## 5.1 Race Types: Circuit, Sprint, Street, Dirt, etc.

*Forza Horizon 6* features a wide variety of race types tailored for different cars, terrains, and player skills. Knowing which car to use — and how to approach each format — is key to success.

Circuit Races

- Closed loops with multiple laps.
- Require precision and consistency on braking zones and corners.
- Appear in all terrain types (asphalt, dirt, snow).
- Best suited for handling-focused builds and racing tires.

Sprint Races

- Point-to-point races from one location to another.
- Often involve a mix of road types and dynamic turns.
- Focus on acceleration, grip, and route knowledge.

Street Races

- Nighttime events with traffic, tight corners, and minimal safety barriers.
- Need strong reflexes and grippy street tires.
- Often tied to rival progression or influence boosts.

Dirt & Cross Country

- Off-road races through forests, rivers, deserts, and farms.

- Best tackled with AWD systems, rally suspension, and off-road tires.
- Terrain can change based on season (mud, snow, ice).

## 5.2 Event Types: Horizon Stories, Showcase, Eliminator

Beyond traditional races, FH6 offers unique, cinematic, and creative events that break up the routine.

Horizon Stories

- Mini-campaigns with voiced characters and themed goals.
- Examples: Drift Academy, Car Culture Chronicles, Midnight Touge Legends.
- Progression rewards unique cars, emotes, and clothing items.
- Scored by stars (1–3 per chapter), with bonuses for style, speed, and precision.

Showcase Events

- Epic one-off races vs. planes, trains, boats, or even giant robots.
- Designed to wow — cinematic intros, custom routes, dramatic finishes.
- Usually unlocked by Festival expansion or story progression.

The Eliminator

- FH's take on a battle royale.
- 30–70 drivers drop into a shrinking arena.

- Find cars on the map (Level 1 to 10), upgrade through head-to-head wins.
- Last driver standing wins after a final showdown sprint.

Custom Blueprints & Community Events

- Players can create/share races with unique conditions: foggy nights, reverse routes, weather chaos.
- Search by tags or creator name for endless new challenges.

## 5.3 Tips for Winning Races and Beating Rivals

You've got the cars — now here's how to dominate every starting grid.

Start Strong

- Use manual + clutch (if skilled) for faster launches.
- Time your acceleration right at the countdown to avoid wheelspin.

Corner Like a Pro

- Use the brake zone indicators, but learn to brake before the red, not inside it.
- Feather the throttle around tight curves, especially on dirt.
- Master trail braking for smoother transitions in tighter corners.

Use Rivals Mode for Practice

- Replay races against "ghosts" of real players or friends.
- Learn alternate lines and discover better braking/boost points.

Tuning for Wins

- Always customize suspension, tire pressure, and final drive for the event type.
- Lower tire pressure = more grip. Higher = faster straight-line speed.

Drivatar Difficulty

- Increase AI level (up to Unbeatable) for better rewards — but test first.
- Some seasonal events require wins on higher difficulties.

## 5.4 XP Boosts, Skill Chains & Influence Points

Progression isn't just about wins — style and stunts matter, too.

Earning XP & Leveling Up

- XP is gained from:
  o Races
  o Stunts (jumps, drifts, skills)
  o Smashing XP boards
  o Completing daily/weekly challenges
- Leveling up grants Wheelspins, Credits, and unlocks new event chains.

Building Skill Chains

- Combine stunts like:
  - Drifts + Near Misses + Air + Jumps + Speed + Burnouts
- Avoid crashing to bank multipliers and earn Skill Points for Car Masteries.

Tip: Use cars with Skill Chain bonuses (check their Mastery Tree).

Influence Points (Campaign Progress)

- Influence fuels Horizon Story progression.
- Earn it via:
  - Events
  - Photo Challenges
  - Showcases
  - Streaming or sharing content via Horizon Life

Boosters & Multiplier Tips

- Festival homes and clothing can sometimes boost XP/Influence gain.
- Skills multiply rapidly in Drift Zones, Danger Signs, and open fields — great for farming.

# CHAPTER 6: TUNING & CUSTOMIZATION

## 6.1 Basic vs. Advanced Tuning

Tuning in FH6 can be as simple or as deep as you want — from basic upgrades to intricate tweaks affecting handling, speed, and terrain grip.

Basic Tuning

- Available via the Upgrades menu.
- Auto-upgrade options (e.g., "Upgrade to S1 Class") make it quick and easy.
- Swap engines, install turbos, adjust suspension types, and more.
- Ideal for beginners looking for quick boosts in performance.

Advanced Tuning

- Accessed via the Tuning & Setup > Custom Tuning menu.
- Lets players control:
  - Tire pressure
  - Gear ratios
  - Alignment (camber, toe, caster)
  - Springs, dampers, anti-roll bars
  - Aero (downforce)
  - Differential behavior

Pro Tip: Save and share your tuning setups — top builds can go viral in the community and earn CR when downloaded.

## 6.2 How to Read and Adjust Car Stats

Understanding what each stat means will help you build smarter cars for specific challenges.

Core Car Stats

| Stat | What It Affects |
|---|---|
| Speed | Top speed on long straights (highways, sprints) |
| Acceleration | How quickly a car gains speed from a stop |
| Launch | Initial take-off (drag, off-road, short sprints) |
| Braking | How quickly a car slows down efficiently |
| Handling | Cornering ability, especially at high speed |
| Offroad | Stability and grip on uneven terrain |

Adjusting for Events

- For drag races, prioritize launch and acceleration.
- For mountain sprints or circuits, focus on handling and braking.
- For cross country or rally, boost off-road and grip.

Use the Dyno Graph

- Found in the tuning menu, shows power curves.
- Great for analyzing where your car makes peak torque and horsepower — useful for adjusting gear ratios and shift points.

## 6.3 Livery Editor: Design and Share Your Look

The Livery Editor is your go-to tool for turning your car into a moving work of art.

How It Works

- Use layers, shapes, text, and logos.
- Apply vinyls to individual parts: hood, roof, sides, rear, etc.
- Can mirror or asymmetrically design left/right sides.

Popular Uses

- Create real-world liveries (e.g., anime, race teams, retro).
- Make unique club branding for online crews.
- Build sponsored rides or memes to go viral.

Sharing & Downloading

- Save and upload designs to the community hub.
- Search by keywords, creator, or car model.
- Earning downloads & likes will net you rewards and followers.

## 6.4 Blueprint Builder: Creating Custom Events

This tool turns every player into a game designer. Create fully custom events using your imagination and in-game tools.

Starting a Blueprint

- Enter a race, then choose "Create Route" or "Event Lab".
- Drive the route you want to use, placing checkpoints or letting it free-flow.

Customization Options

- Adjust:
    o Time of day
    o Weather conditions
    o Traffic and Drivatars
    o Vehicle restrictions
    o Music, intro cameras, and effects
- Add props like ramps, tunnels, billboards, flaming rings, etc.

Event Lab 2.0

- FH6 adds more tools: animated objects, moving platforms, sound triggers.
- You can now script mini-missions, stunts, or even puzzles.

Publishing & Sharing

- Upload with tags like:
    o "Drift track"
    o "Mini-game"
    o "Story mode"
- Share the event code with friends or make it public.
- Track plays, likes, and remixes.

# CHAPTER 7: MULTIPLAYER & ONLINE MODES

## 7.1 Horizon Open, Convoys, and Clubs

*Forza Horizon 6* brings players together across its massive open world through both casual and competitive modes. Here's how to squad up, join communities, and dive into the action.

Horizon Open

- Open-world multiplayer races and events — no matchmaking restrictions.
- Includes:
    o Open Racing – Road, dirt, cross country, street.
    o Drift – Compete in drift zones head-to-head.
    o Playground Games – Team-based minigames like King, Flag Rush, and Infected.
    o Custom Racing – Create and join lobbies with specific restrictions.

Pro Tip: Horizon Open is great for earning Influence, Wheelspins, and checking off Playlist objectives.

Convoys

- Temporary or permanent groups of friends you can explore and race with.
- Members appear synced on the map and can fast travel to each other.
- Ideal for road trips, co-op challenges, and quick event coordination.

Clubs

- Persistent communities — like racing guilds.
- Join public or private clubs based on skill, theme, or vibe.
- Club features:
  - Weekly leaderboards (XP contribution)
  - Shared tags and branding
  - Club-only filters for livery sharing and event blueprints

## 7.2 PvP vs. Co-op Strategies

Whether you're racing against strangers or teaming up with friends, knowing the right strategy makes all the difference.

PvP (Player vs. Player) Tips

- Know your class meta – Some PI classes are more competitive (e.g., A800 and S1900).
- Use ghosting to your advantage – Most Horizon Open races use ghost mode for the first 10 seconds; use it to cleanly break away.
- Brake early, not late – Human players are unpredictable. Defensive driving often wins.
- Avoid walls – Unlike AI, real players don't slow down when they crash. One mistake can end your run.

Meta Insight: AWD builds with high acceleration tend to dominate early in races — great for quick points in Horizon Open.

Co-op Mode Tips

- Available in:
  - Seasonal Championships
  - Story Events
  - Horizon Arcade
- Race with friends vs. AI for better odds at winning Playlist rewards.
- Communicate roles — who's tackling objectives, who's defending flags, etc.
- Use voice chat or Quick Chat to stay coordinated.

Eliminator Co-op Strategy (Unofficial)

- While it's a solo mode, some players team up off-mic or with friends in free roam to share info and dominate showdowns.
- Tip: Use location pings and shadowing to block opponents during final races.

## 7.3 Best Cars for Online Play

Online play in *Forza Horizon 6* is all about choosing the right car for the job — cars that balance speed, grip, and adaptability under pressure. Here are some class-specific champions that shine online.

A-Class (A800) – Balanced Mastery

- Subaru WRX STI '15 (AWD build) – Great for mixed surface.

- Honda NSX-R '92 (grip build) – Lightweight and surgical handling.
- Ford Escort RS Cosworth – Excellent off-road grip and acceleration.

Perfect for open racing and co-op where flexibility is key.

S1-Class (S1900) – The Online Sweet Spot

- Toyota Supra RZ '98 (AWD swap) – Top-tier speed & grip.
- Lamborghini Huracán LP 610-4 – All-rounder with strong top-end.
- Audi RS6 Avant – Sleeper wagon with torque and stability.

Most Horizon Open races live in S1 — ideal for street & road domination.

S2-Class (S2998) – Speed Demons

- Koenigsegg Jesko – Brutal speed, crazy downforce, tough to tame.
- Aston Martin Vulcan AMR Pro – Better control for tight tracks.
- Bugatti Divo – Great for long sprints and leaderboards.

Online Tip: Use community tune search terms like "Meta", "Online PvP", or "Anti-wall" for optimized builds.


## 7.4 Seasonal Events & Leaderboard Climbing

Every week, FH6 updates with new challenges, races, and leaderboard grinds through its Festival Playlist.

## What Are Seasonal Events?

- Weekly rotating objectives tied to:
    - Races (Road, Dirt, Cross-Country, Street)
    - PR Stunts (Speed Zones, Danger Signs, Drift Zones)
    - Horizon Arcade
    - Photo, Treasure, and Collectible Challenges
- Completing earns points toward seasonal rewards (cars, clothing, credits).

## How to Dominate the Playlist

- Check requirements early – Cars and tuning restrictions vary weekly.
- Tune cars for the event – A PI maxed-out car isn't always the best; balance is key.
- Do co-op races for easier wins vs AI and more Playlist points.

## Climbing the Leaderboards

- Each PR Stunt (e.g., Drift Zones, Speed Zones) has a global leaderboard.
- Use RWD drift builds or high-speed monsters to place top 1%.
- Utilize rewind tactically to perfect corners.

Leaderboard Pro Tip: Top players adjust weather conditions, car height, tire pressure, and use rewind + ghost runs for surgical attempts.

## Rewards & Prestige

- Climbing leaderboards and completing full seasons unlocks:
    - Rare and exclusive cars
    - Legendary status
    - Club bragging rights
    - In-game accolades, badges, and profile effects

Weekly Goal: Aim for 40–60 Playlist points each week to unlock both seasonal reward cars.

# CHAPTER 8: SEASONAL CHALLENGES AND REWARDS

## 8.1 Understanding the Festival Playlist

The Festival Playlist is your seasonal roadmap in FH6 —
combining single-player, co-op, and online activities with a
rewarding progression system tied to the in-game economy.

What Is the Festival Playlist?

- A rotating 4-week season cycle (Spring, Summer, Autumn, Winter)
- Each week (season) offers:
  o Unique cars
  o Clothing & cosmetics
  o Wheelspins and Credits
  o Community challenges (Photos, Treasure Hunts)
- Points earned from events contribute toward seasonal and series-long rewards.

Why It Matters

- Essential for unlocking exclusive vehicles not available in the Autoshow or Auction House.
- Driving force behind player engagement and long-term goals.
- Often includes limited-time challenges with high payouts.

How It Impacts the Economy

- Provides steady income through CR, XP, and Forzathon Points.
- High Playlist completion = VIP reputation with clubs and community creators.
- Incentivizes variety in gameplay: from off-road racing to creative blueprints.

Goal: Complete at least 40–60 points per week to unlock both seasonal reward cars (usually a Rare + Epic or Legendary).


## 8.2 Weekly and Monthly Tasks Explained

Each season contains a blend of activities broken down into weekly and monthly categories, each affecting your rewards and leaderboard progress.

Weekly Tasks (Reset Every 7 Days)

- Seasonal Championships – 3-race events against AI or with friends.
- PR Stunts – Speed Zones, Danger Signs, Drift Zones.
- Photo Challenges – Snap a specific car or scene.
- Horizon Arcade or Co-Op Races
- Treasure Hunts & Collectibles – Solve riddles, destroy objects.
- The Trial – A high-difficulty team vs. AI challenge (offers huge rewards).
- Seasonal Events – Playlist-specific Horizon Stories or Showcases.

Reset Time: Every Thursday, global reset time syncs with player time zone.

Monthly Tasks (Reset Every 4 Weeks)

- Monthly Rivals – Beat ghost times on set tracks using stock cars.
- Forza EV Events – Focus on electric cars and clean driving.
- Online Tour – Complete races with live players for points and badges.

Reward Structure

- Points per event usually range from 1–10, with full-season rewards requiring ~60 points.
- Extra points can be earned by:
    o Owning DLC cars
    o Completing in higher difficulty tiers
    o Submitting designs, blueprints, or tunes

## 8.3 Rare Cars and Unlockables from Seasons

Some of the most sought-after cars in *Forza Horizon 6* can only be acquired through seasonal events or timed objectives — making them valuable in the economy and high-demand in the Auction House.

Types of Seasonal Unlocks

- Exclusive Reward Cars: Only obtainable via the Festival Playlist.
    o Examples: Ferrari F355 Challenge, Ford Supervan 4, Toyota Celica GT-Four ST205.

- Return of Legacy Rides: Classic Forza favorites that were previously vaulted.
- Themed Vehicles: Based on seasonal events or holidays (e.g. Halloween muscle cars, Winter rally beasts).

Tracking What's Rare

- Legendary Tier cars are marked gold in your garage.
- Auction House shows demand via price cap and bidding volume.
- Some rare cars only appear once per Series — be alert during Playlist previews.

Other Unlockables

- Emotes, Horns & Cosmetics – Often limited-time, themed to the season.
- Exclusive Rims, Wings, and Body Kits
- Super Wheelspins – Award large CR sums or Legendary cosmetics.

## 8.4 Efficient Farming Strategies

Whether you're grinding for CR, XP, or skill points, efficiency is key. Here's how to build up your bank and garage smart — not hard.

Credit Farming

- Goliath AFK Races: Create a 50-lap Goliath with no opponents. Rubber band your controller, let it ride.

- Super Wheelspins: Farm skill points via drift or speed traps, convert them into spins through specific cars (e.g., *Jeep Trailcat* or *Toyota Supra* skill trees).
- Auction Flipping: Buy underpriced rares, tune them, then resell for profit — especially after a seasonal car goes out of rotation.

Fastest Farm: Combine Goliath + Super Wheelspin builds. You'll gain CR, skill points, and spins all at once.

XP & Skill Point Farming

- Use cars with maxed skill chains, like the Hoonicorn V2 or Formula Drift 599.
- Hit speed zones and drift zones repeatedly in skill multiplier zones (e.g. airport, mountain roads).
- Stack skills with active perks like "Skill Legend" and "Extra Life."

Use Blueprint Races labeled "Skill Point Farm" — community-made tracks that give max points in under 3 minutes.

Seasonal Playlist Efficiency

- Knock out Photo, Arcade, and Collectible Challenges first (easy points).
- Use Co-op to breeze through championships.
- Save hard stuff like The Trial for last, or do it with friends to reduce frustration.

# CHAPTER 9: COLLECTIBLES AND SECRETS

## 9.1 Barn Finds and Treasure Hunts

Barn Finds and Treasure Hunts add mystery and excitement to the *Forza Horizon 6* experience, rewarding players with hidden cars and collectibles.

Barn Finds: Unlocking Hidden Cars

- How It Works: Throughout the map, you'll receive clues or whispers from characters that point to hidden barns containing classic or rare cars.
    - Use clues provided in the "Barn Find" screen to locate specific barns.
    - Completing a Barn Find unlocks the car for your garage, and it's often a rare or classic vehicle you can't get elsewhere.

Barn Find Cars

- Some iconic vehicles found in Barns include:
    - Volkswagen Type 2 Bus – A popular and quirky classic.
    - Shelby Cobra 427 – A powerhouse muscle car.
    - Mazda RX-7 Spirit R – An iconic JDM car.

Treasure Hunts: Solving Riddles

- Clue System: Players are given cryptic clues that lead to hidden treasure boxes. Unlocking these will grant rewards like CR, Super Wheelspins, and sometimes rare cars.
  - For example, a clue might refer to a certain landmark or a color of a car in your inventory.
- Treasure Hunt Locations: These treasures can be found in remote or hard-to-reach areas of the map, adding extra exploration to the game.

## 9.2 Bonus Boards & Danger Signs

These activities not only increase your car's skills but are also fantastic for collecting bonuses and progressing your overall stats.

Bonus Boards: Skill Points & XP

- Location: Spread across the map, these boards give XP and Skill Points when destroyed.
- Types of Bonus Boards:
  - XP Boards: Offer a large amount of XP.
  - Skill Boards: Award Skill Points used to unlock car perks and improve your vehicles.
  - Fast Travel Boards: Once collected, they reduce the cost of Fast Travel across the map, making your journey more efficient.

Danger Signs: Stunt Jumps

- How It Works: Danger Signs are huge ramps or jumps placed across the map. Your goal is to launch your car off them and achieve the longest distance or height possible.

- Tips for Success:
    - Use Offroad Cars: Some jumps are easier with vehicles that have high suspension and off-road tuning.
    - Max Out Speed: Make sure you're at the right speed before hitting the ramp for maximum airtime.

Danger Sign Pro Tip: Build up your car's speed using nearby roads and environments (like downhill terrain) for a better shot at achieving that perfect jump distance.

## 9.3 Photo Challenges and Vista Locations

The photo challenges and Vista Locations are perfect for creative players looking to capture the beauty of the Horizon Festival's world.

Photo Challenges

- Challenge Overview: You'll be tasked with taking pictures of specific cars in specific locations, with additional conditions like a time of day or weather.
    - Examples: "Take a photo of an AWD car at sunset near the ocean" or "Capture a picture of a muscle car at the speed trap."
- Reward: Completing these challenges will net you CR, XP, and occasionally, exclusive items or cars.

Vista Locations

- Locations of Beauty: These are picturesque viewpoints around the map, perfect for taking snapshots of your favorite cars.
    - Some vistas are also tied to seasonal challenges, requiring you to visit and capture the beauty of certain locations.
    - Unlock: Visiting each Vista unlocks a unique achievement or gives a bonus to your collection.

Pro Tip: The best time to take photos is during the Golden Hour (early morning or sunset) for natural lighting effects.

## 9.4 Achievements and Hidden Trophies

Achievement hunting is a great way to deepen your engagement with *Forza Horizon 6* and unlock hidden content.

Standard Achievements

- Examples:
    - *"Legendary Racer"*: Complete all Horizon Festival challenges.
    - *"The Collector"*: Own 100 cars.
    - *"Champion of Horizon"*: Win every Seasonal Championship at least once.

Hidden Trophies

- These are achievements not immediately visible in the game's list.
- Hidden trophies require players to explore the game fully, often including:

- Completing special story missions.
- Earning all collectible items (bonus boards, barn finds, vistas).
- Hitting specific milestones (e.g., winning 100 races).

Unlocking Secrets

- Hidden achievements often lead to exclusive cars or rare gear.
- Players often share hidden achievements and how to unlock them in the community, so keep an eye on Forza forums and social media!

Secret Achievement Tip: Some secret trophies require you to complete all seasonal content in one Series (4 weeks), so focus on doing everything before the reset.

# CHAPTER 10: PRO TIPS & MASTER STRATEGIES

## 10.1 Drivatar AI: How to Outsmart Them

The AI in *Forza Horizon 6*, known as Drivatars, are designed to simulate real human behavior in races. Understanding how to exploit their weaknesses can give you a competitive edge.

Understanding Drivatars

- Behavior: Drivatars have varying levels of aggression, skill, and unpredictability. They mirror player tendencies but are often predictable in certain situations.
    - Aggressive Drivatars will dive for corners and block you when trying to pass.
    - Defensive Drivatars take wider lines and focus on maintaining their position.

How to Outsmart Them

- Cornering: Drivatars tend to brake too early or too late in turns. Use this to your advantage:
    - Brake late, letting them overshoot, then pass them on the inside.
    - If a Drivatar takes a wide line, you can cut across and take the corner faster.
- Defending and Attacking:
    - Don't be predictable: Drivatars learn your tactics and adapt. Mix up your cornering techniques, from taking tight lines to wide ones to throw them off.

- o Feints: If you're being followed, break hard at the last moment and take a sharp turn. Drivatars may follow your old line, giving you a chance to break away.

Pro Tip: Drivatars can be "tricked" into slowing down by making sudden changes in your driving style, such as driving on the grass or dirt for a moment, then quickly regaining the track.

## 10.2 Drift Zones & Speed Traps Mastery

Mastering Drift Zones and Speed Traps is crucial for both completing the Festival Playlist and for leaderboard success. Here's how to perfect your technique for these two key activities.

Drift Zones

- Understanding Drift Zones: These are sections of the map where you need to maintain continuous drifting through a marked area. Points are awarded for the length of your drift, angle, and style.

How to Maximize Drift Scores

- Choose the Right Car: Cars with a rear-wheel-drive (RWD) configuration are typically best for drifting. Look for lightweight, high-horsepower cars (e.g., Ford Mustang GT350, BMW M4).
- Tune for Drifting: Optimize your car for drift:
  - o Adjust tire pressure (lower for easier drift initiation).
  - o Increase the rear wing for more rear-end stability.

- o Set suspension soft to maximize the car's handling in turns.
- The Right Technique:
  - o Initiate a drift early before entering the zone. For more precision, use the e-brake to start the drift and control it by modulating the throttle.
  - o Maintain a steady angle and don't overcorrect. Oversteering wastes valuable time and points.
- Drift Zone Tips:
  - o Look for long, sweeping corners that allow you to build your drift angle without sharp turns disrupting your flow.
  - o If you have a hard time keeping control, use drift assists until you're comfortable.

Pro Tip: In tougher drift zones, it's often more efficient to sacrifice speed for angle to build a high combo chain, rather than rushing through the zone.

Speed Traps

- What Are Speed Traps?: Speed Traps are sections where you must pass through at the highest speed possible. Time your approach perfectly to hit the highest possible score.

How to Master Speed Traps

- Choose the Right Car: Use a high-speed car that has good acceleration and handling at top speeds, like the Bugatti Chiron or Aston Martin DBS Superleggera.
- Tuning for Top Speed:
  - o Maximize aerodynamics: Lower downforce (front and rear) to reduce drag.

- Maximize engine performance: Use cars with high horsepower and high gearing for straight-line speed.
- Use gear ratios: Set up longer gear ratios, so your car stays in its optimal power band at high speeds.
- Approach Strategy:
  - Start with a wide approach and build speed gradually, hitting the Speed Trap at full throttle.
  - Avoid sharp turns right before the trap; you need a clean, uninterrupted line into the trap.
- Perfecting Speed Trap Runs:
  - Speed Zones Before the Trap: Use high-speed sections of the track to build momentum, avoiding unnecessary slowdowns.
  - Drafting: If you're near other cars, using their draft to gain extra speed can significantly help.

Speed Tip: Boost your performance on Speed Traps by using Nitrous or Turbo boosts right before crossing the trap for that extra push.

## 10.3 Ultimate Credits and XP Farming Techniques

Efficiently farming Credits (CR) and XP is essential for progressing through *Forza Horizon 6* and unlocking cars, cosmetics, and upgrades. Here's how to maximize your earnings without feeling like you're grinding too much.

Maximizing Credit (CR) Farming

- AFK Goliath Races: The Goliath is the longest race in *Forza Horizon 6*, and while completing it manually can take a long time, you can set it up as an AFK race to earn Credits while you're away.

- o Use a rubber band or controller macro to hold your car on a steady path (e.g., straight roads), allowing you to complete the race without actively driving.
- o Ensure your car is at the correct class and difficulty level to make the race efficient.
- Auction House Flipping: Buying rare cars from the Auction House at underpriced rates and reselling them can be incredibly profitable, especially after the car is no longer available in the current Festival Playlist or is a seasonal reward.
  - o Focus on flipping cars that are popular or have niche appeal. The community often shares tips on the hot cars to buy and sell.
- Car Meets & Horizon Arcade: Completing challenges at Horizon Arcade not only provides XP but can be done in multiplayer with friends for even more rewards. Teaming up in Car Meets also helps you unlock more items while earning consistent CR and XP.
  - o Pay attention to the bonus boards, as many can be used to double down on your efforts (e.g., completing skill boards alongside other activities).
- Skill Point Farming: Use Skill Points to unlock perks for your cars, and focus on skill point farming:
  - o Drift Zones and Speed Zones can be excellent sources of skill points.
  - o Certain cars with good skill trees, such as the Chevrolet Camaro Forza Edition, grant skill multipliers that increase the efficiency of your farming.

Farming Tip: Use your highest-performance car to farm the most lucrative races and activities. Don't forget about Super Wheelspin rewards — they offer the potential for large CR bonuses and car unlocks.

Maximizing XP Farming

- XP Boosts: Start by unlocking XP Boosts through your Car Mastery and Skill Trees. Some vehicles grant XP Boosts after completing a set of challenges or leveling up specific skills.
- Horizon Arcade: Participate in Horizon Arcade events where you can earn XP quickly by completing a variety of challenges. These can be repetitive but rewarding.
- Speed Zones and Drift Zones: Speed Zones, where you need to beat speed records, and Drift Zones provide excellent XP and Skill Points.
- Race Championships: Focus on high-difficulty seasonal events, especially those that offer large XP rewards. Completing championships and timed events ensures a substantial XP gain.

Pro Tip: Combine high-reward, low-effort activities like Seasonal Events with long-term activities such as AFK Goliath runs for the most effective farming strategy.

## 10.4 Preparing for Competitive Play and Future Expansions

The competitive side of *Forza Horizon 6* offers players a chance to test their skills against others in online races, clubs, and ranked events. This section will cover how to prepare for high-level play and stay ahead of future expansions and updates.

Competitive Play: Getting Ready for Online Events

- Car Tuning for Multiplayer:
    - Multiplayer races require fine-tuned cars that are optimal for different race conditions. Track-tuned cars are designed for higher speeds and handling, while off-road builds are needed for cross-country events.
    - Tune your car for the specific event type (road races, dirt races, etc.) by adjusting tire pressures, suspension, weight distribution, and gearing.
- Understanding the Leaderboards: In competitive play, ranking high requires consistency:
    - Participate regularly in multiplayer races and ranked events to increase your skill level.
    - Focus on points, not just wins. Completing objectives like clean laps, drift points, or passing a set number of players will boost your overall standing.
- Creating a Winning Strategy:
    - Learn the tracks and events you are participating in. Map out your racing strategy (e.g., learning where Drivatars tend to make mistakes or where speed boosts are located).
    - Practice car control, especially with high-performance vehicles that you intend to use in competitive races.

Pro Tip: In online events, the competition can get fierce. Stay ahead by keeping your car well-tuned for specific race conditions, and study other players' tactics to gain an advantage.

Preparing for Expansions and Future Content

- *Forza Horizon 6* will likely feature future expansions, including new locations, cars, and challenges. Here's how to stay ready:
    - DLC & Expansion Pass: Make sure you have the Expansion Pass for access to future expansions. Some of the best cars and tracks come with these downloadable packs.
    - Keep Your Garage Ready: Stockpile credits and rare cars that are set to become more valuable with upcoming updates. Classic cars and limited-time vehicles often become more rare as new content is released.
    - Event Previews: Keep an eye on official *Forza Horizon* channels and the Festival Playlist for hints about upcoming expansions or seasonal content. Being informed means you can plan ahead for what's coming.

Expansion Tip: Once expansions are announced, start grinding specific event types related to the new content (e.g., if the expansion adds more off-road events, prepare by collecting and tuning off-road vehicles).

www.ingramcontent.com/pod-product-compliance
Lightning Source LLC
LaVergne TN
LVHW051613050326
832903LV00033B/4471